D1217303

MONSTERS OF THE ANIMAL KINGDOM

TARANTULAS

Rachel Lynette

PowerKiDS press™

New York

For David

Published in 2013 by The Rosen Publishing Group, Inc.
29 East 21st Street, New York, NY 10010

First Edition

Editor: Jennifer Way
Book Design: Greg Tucker

Photo Credits: Cover, pp. 12–13 Danita Delimont/Gallo Images/Getty Images; p. 4 worldwildlifewonders/Shutterstock.com; pp. 5 (left), 7, 9, 15 Cathy Keifer/Shutterstock.com; p. 5 (bottom) Audrey Snider-Bell/Shutterstock.com; p. 6 Brian Lasenby/Shutterstock.com; p. 8 Dr. Morley Read/Shutterstock.com; p. 10 312010/Shutterstock.com; p. 11 John S. Mitchell/Oxford Scientific/Getty Images; p. 14 Kate Thompson/National Geographic/Getty Images; p. 16 Dirk Ercken/Shutterstock.com; p. 17 (top) Tom McHugh/Photo Researchers/Getty Images; p. 17 (bottom) John Cancalosi/Peter Arnold/Getty Images; p. 18 StaceyD_KS/Shutterstock.com; p. 19 Creatista/Shutterstock.com; p. 20 Robert Oelman/Oxford Scientific/Getty Images; p. 21 Hemera Technologies/PhotoObjects.net/Thinkstock; p. 22 Mark D. Callanan/Photolibrary/Getty Images.

Library of Congress Cataloging-in-Publication Data

Lynette, Rachel.
Tarantulas / by Rachel Lynette. — 1st ed.
    p. cm. — (Monsters of the animal kingdom)
Includes index.
ISBN 978-1-4488-9632-5 (library binding) — ISBN 978-1-4488-9720-9 (pbk.) —
ISBN 978-1-4488-9721-6 (6-pack)
1. Tarantulas—Juvenile literature. I. Title.
QL458.42.T5L96 2013
595.4'4—dc23
                        2012017448

Manufactured in the United States of America

CPSIA Compliance Information: Batch #W13PK5: For Further Information contact Rosen Publishing, New York, New York at 1-800-237-9932

CONTENTS

TERRIFYING TARANTULAS

Can you imagine seeing a spider as big as a dinner plate? At 12 inches (30 cm) across, the Goliath bird-eating tarantula is one of the biggest spiders on the planet! Most tarantulas are not nearly that large, though. In fact, some kinds of tarantulas are smaller than your fingernail. Tarantulas may look scary, but they rarely hurt people.

The zebra tarantula, shown here, grows to about 5 inches (13 cm) across. It lives in Costa Rica.

Left: The greenbottle blue tarantula is known for its striking color. This spider can be found in Venezuela. *Below*: Here is a Goliath bird-eating tarantula. It is the second-biggest spider on Earth, although it is the world's biggest in terms of body mass.

All tarantulas are spiders. There are more than 37,500 different **species** of spiders in the world. About 850 of these species are tarantulas. Around 30 of those species can be found in the warmer parts of North America, including California, Arizona, and New Mexico.

ulas can be found on every continent except
a. Tarantulas live only in areas that have warm
. There are more tarantulas on the continent of
merica than anywhere else.

tarantulas live in underground **burrows** that
themselves. They spin silk to line their burrows.

-kneed tarantula is
e opening of its burrow.

Here an orange baboon tarantula has spun a web around its burrow.

These burrows can be up to 6 feet (2 m) deep! Other tarantulas live in trees. They spin silk tubes that stretch between leaves or make hammock-shaped nests. Some tarantulas move from place to place. They find shelter wherever they can. That could be under rocks, in hollow logs, or even in another spider's abandoned burrow.

EIGHT HAIRY LEGS!

Like all spiders, tarantulas have eight legs and two main body parts. All eight legs are attached to the front part of the body. This front section of the body also contains the tarantula's brain, jaws, eyes, and stomach. The back body part is called the **abdomen**. The abdomen contains the guts, heart, lungs, and silk **glands**.

In this picture, you can see the tarantula's abdomen and the front section below it, as well as its eight legs.

In this close-up shot of a greenbottle blue tarantula, you can see the hairs that cover its body.

A tarantula's legs and body are covered with hairs. These sensitive hairs help the tarantula sense movement and heat. Some tarantulas have special, barbed hairs that help protect them from **predators**. The hairs hurt the predator's skin and eyes and sometimes scare the animal away.

BUILT FOR BITING

Many people are afraid of being bitten by a tarantula. Tarantulas are **venomous**, but a tarantula's venom is not nearly strong enough to kill a human. A tarantula's venom comes from a gland behind its mouth. It flows through the tarantula's sharp fangs to poison its **prey**. Even though tarantulas have eight eyes, they are

You can see the short, leg-like pedipalps of this Mexican red-kneed tarantula on the lower left side of the animal.

This king baboon tarantula has its pedipalps raised, and you can see its fangs.

good only for sensing light and dark. Tarantulas have two small, leg-like parts near their mouths called **pedipalps**. They use their pedipalps to sense objects and to find food. They also use their pedipalps to catch and to hold their prey.

SCARY FACTS

1 **Mating** is risky business for a male tarantula. The female may decide to eat the male!

2 Baby tarantulas eat their way out of their eggs. They may also eat some of their siblings soon after they are born.

3 Tarantulas are most in danger when they are **molting**. After they leave the old **exoskeleton**, they must wait several hours for the new one to harden.

4 The Goliath bird-eating spider can have fangs up to 1 inch (2.5 cm) long!

5 Some kinds of tarantulas lay a line of silk in front of their burrows. The line alerts the tarantula when an animal bumps into it.

6 In the 1955 horror movie *Tarantula*, a giant tarantula escapes from a science lab and terrifies the people in the nearby town.

7 In the video game *Deadly Creatures*, you can play as either a scorpion or a tarantula as you fight lizards, wasps, and even humans.

8 An Italian legend says that if a tarantula bites a woman, she will fall into a trance that can be cured only by dancing.

MOLTING

Tarantulas do not have bones, as you do. Instead, they have hard exoskeletons. The exoskeleton protects the tarantula like a suit of armor. A young tarantula will outgrow its exoskeleton several times before it is full grown. When this happens, the tarantula molts by crawling out of its old exoskeleton. The new exoskeleton is already grown underneath the old one!

Molting makes tarantulas sluggish and easier to attack. Because of this, they may seek protected spots, where they can be safer.

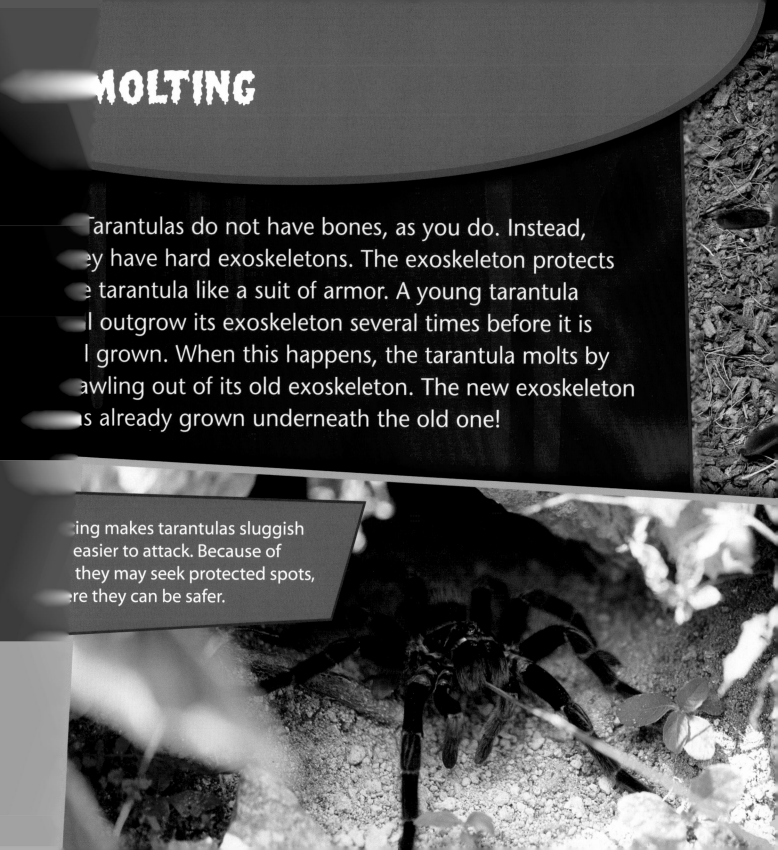

A tarantula that has lost a leg can often grow a new one. The leg grows folded under the exoskeleton. When the tarantula next molts, it will have a new leg, although it is often smaller than the other legs.

This tarantula is in the middle of molting. You can see its old exoskeleton in the lower left corner. After it has been shed, the spider must wait for its fangs and new exoskeleton to harden.

A LIQUID DIET

Tarantulas hunt at night. They are **carnivores** and will eat any animal they can catch. This can include insects, other kinds of spiders, small lizards, mice, snakes, frogs, and even birds.

When the tarantula senses that prey is nearby, it will attack by pouncing on the animal and sinking its fangs

Here a tarantula is eating a tree frog.

Above: This tarantula has captured a snake for its dinner. *Below*: Tarantulas generally hide out and wait for prey to come near them so they can attack. Animals that hunt this way are called ambush predators.

into the animal's body. The venom from the tarantula's fangs stops the animal from moving. Then the tarantula drips its own **digestive juices** into the animal's body. The juices turn the animal's insides into a gooey liquid that the tarantula sucks into its stomach.

BABY TARANTULAS

Tarantulas live alone, except when they are mating. Tarantulas can mate when they are around nine years old. After mating, the female spins a soft egg sac. She fills it with up to 1,000 eggs. She puts the sac in a safe place or carries it with her on her back. The eggs hatch after about seven weeks.

These newly hatched spiderlings, or baby spiders, are resting on their mother. They will go off on their own after their first molt.

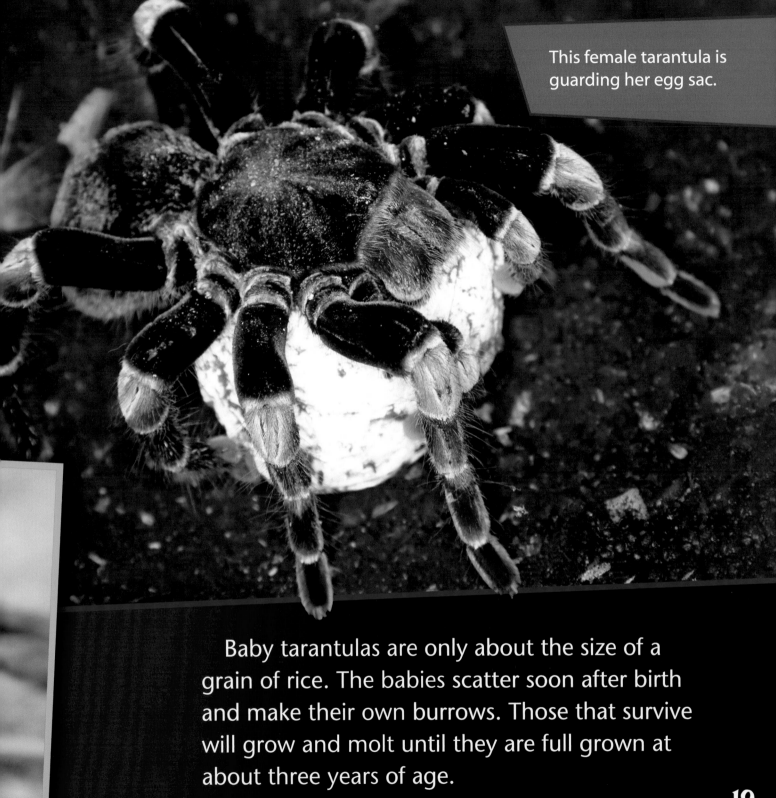

Baby tarantulas are only about the size of a grain of rice. The babies scatter soon after birth and make their own burrows. Those that survive will grow and molt until they are full grown at about three years of age.

TARANTULAS FOR DINNER

Tarantulas have many predators, including lizards, birds, snakes, skunks, and weasels. In some countries, such as Cambodia, humans also eat tarantulas. Tarantulas often try to scare predators away by standing upright on their back two legs to make themselves look bigger.

The tarantula hawk, shown here, is a type of wasp that is found in Asia, Africa, Australia, North America, and South America.

This tarantula hawk is stalking a tarantula. The wasp will drag the tarantula into its burrow, where it will lay an egg on the spider.

Very unlucky tarantulas become prey to a large wasp called the tarantula hawk. First, the tarantula hawk stings the tarantula, which stops the spider from moving. Then it lays an egg on the tarantula's stomach and buries it. When the baby wasp hatches, it will burrow into the still-living tarantula and eat it

TARANTULAS IN DANGER

Only two species of tarantulas are in danger of **extinction**. However, many tarantulas are threatened by loss of habitat, as humans log more forests and build more farms and cities.

Some types of tarantulas are also becoming less common in the wild because they are being illegally hunted and sold as pets. Although they are not very cuddly, tarantulas do make good pets for people who know how to take care of them properly.

People who keep pet tarantulas must learn how to handle them safely. This is important for the spider's health as well as for its owner's.

GLOSSARY

abdomen (AB-duh-mun) The large, rear part of a spider's body.

burrows (BUR-ohz) Holes animals dig in the ground for shelter.

carnivores (KAHR-neh-vorz) Animals that eat only other animals.

digestive juices (dy-JES-tiv JOO-sez) Liquids in the body used to break down food so the body can use it.

exoskeleton (ek-soh-SKEH-leh-tun) The hard covering on the outside of an animal's body that holds and guards the soft insides.

extinction (ek-STINGK-shun) The state of no longer existing.

glands (GLANDZ) Organs or parts of the body that produce elements to help with bodily functions.

mating (MAYT-ing) Coming together to make babies.

molting (MOHLT-ing) Shedding hair, feathers, shell, horns, or an exoskeleton.

pedipalps (PEH-duh-palps) Small, leg-like parts near an arachnid's mouth.

predators (PREH-duh-terz) Animals that kill other animals for food.

prey (PRAY) An animal that is hunted by another animal for food.

species (SPEE-sheez) One kind of living thing. All people are one species.

venomous (VEH-nuh-mis) Having a poisonous bite.

INDEX

WEBSITES

Due to the changing nature of Internet links, PowerKids Press has developed an online list of websites related to the subject of this book. This site is updated regularly. Please use this link to access the list: www.powerkidslinks.com/mak/taran/